QUILTS

Christine Stevens

Department of Farming, Crafts and Cultural Life,
Welsh Folk Museum

GOMER PRESS IN ASSOCIATION WITH THE NATIONAL MUSEUM OF WALES

1993

© National Museum of Wales, 1993

ISBN: 0 86383 941 X

Drawings by J. R. Jenkins and A. Bond

Printed by J. D. Lewis and Sons Ltd.,
Gomer Press, Llandysul, Dyfed

PREFACE

The foundations for the Welsh Folk Museum collection of quilts were laid during the 1930s by the late Ffransis G. Payne, then Assistant Keeper of the Department of Folk Culture and Industries at the National Museum of Wales. Although a few examples of quilts had been donated to the Museum in 1914, no systematic collecting had been undertaken prior to the establishment of the Department in 1932.

The quilting revival of the 1930s caused a new awareness of the quality and workmanship of the many old quilts and patchwork coverlets which existed in Welsh homes. Some of the best specimens in the museum collection were acquired during this pre-war period. During the years immediately after the war, there were attempts to resuscitate interest in quilting and the collection continued to grow, especially after the Quilting Conference of 1950 and Exhibition of 1951 (both held at the Welsh Folk Museum).

There are now over two hundred examples of quilting and patchwork in the collection, dating from the eighteenth up to the middle of the twentieth century. Most are carefully stored on large rollers in the museum, but a selection has been placed in a study room, which may be viewed by appointment.

With this booklet, it is hoped to give a brief introduction to the history of quilting in general, relating this to the development of quilting in Wales, as well as providing an easily accessible source of illustrations of quilts and coverlets in the Welsh Folk Museum collection.

EARLY HISTORY

A quilt consists of two outer layers of fabric with an inner layer of padding, which is held in position by means of decorative stitching. The technique is of considerable antiquity and is known not only throughout Europe, but also in Far Eastern and Middle Eastern countries.

Although the most common surviving quilted items are bedcovers, many of the earliest British records of quilting refer in fact to articles of clothing and armour. Padded and quilted doublets were worn beneath metal armour, and similar garments were even worn instead of armour by light troops, such as archers. One of the few such garments to have survived is a mid-fourteenth century sleeveless doublet of simple linear quilting, reputed to have been worn by Edward Prince of Wales (The Black Prince). A copy is displayed near his tomb in Canterbury Cathedral.

During the fourteenth and fifteenth centuries, the doublet also became a fashionable garment for outer wear. The quilting on these garments remained very simple, usually linear, but much richer materials were used. A particularly fine example survives in the collections of the Musée Historique des Tissus in Lyons, this is a long-sleeved, tight-fitting jacket, in a richly patterned fabric, well-padded, and quilted in lines following the construction of the garment.

The earliest Welsh reference to quilting appears in an inventory of Powys Castle dated 1551, it includes 'a guylte doublet of changeable color, taffata', as well as various bed quilts. One of 'redd sylke' is obviously a coverlet, but at this period underquilts were also much used. A list of the possessions of Sir Gelli Meyrick of Presteigne in Powys, compiled after his execution at Tyburn in 1600, does not differentiate between quilts and mattresses.

During the Elizabethan period, coverlet quilts were the preserve of the upper classes, woollen blankets being generally used as bed coverings. The inventory of Carew Castle, in Dyfed, dated 1592, lists various grand bedding, including embroidered and lace-trimmed velvet hangings and a 'quilt of yellow sercnet, . . . a changeable silke quilt . . . [and] an old black and white silke quilt'. Sarsenet is a very fine soft silk, frequently used for quilting.

It is difficult to discover whether, at this time, quilting was done by the ladies of the household, their servants, or professional quilt makers. Other decorative needlework, such as embroidery, was certainly a lady's occupation, though professional embroiderers did exist. The provision of household linen and furnishing was the province of the lady of the house and her needlewomen. It was quite usual for the spinning and weaving of flax and wool to be undertaken in the home, as well as the making of garments, hangings and bed coverings. From the sixteenth century onwards many of these items were quilted and were presumably produced within the household. However, there is documentary evidence of at least some items of clothing being purchased. An inventory of the contents of Wynnstay in Powys, taken in 1683-84, lists a quantity of clothing 'bought at London and elsewhere in June and July '84' which includes three quilted caps among the cravats, ruffles and waistcoats. The purchase of 'a quilt cap', price two shillings, was also made for Sir Thomas Myddelton of Chirk in 1669. These were probably nightcaps, although quilted and embroidered day caps were worn by men at this time.

The use of quilting increased generally during the seventeenth century, not only for men's and babies' caps, but other items of fashionable clothing such as jackets and waistcoats for both men and women, and elaborate petticoats. John Evelyn in *The Mode* (1661) describes petticoats 'quilted white and red, with broad Flanders lace below'. Quilted clothing and lengths of quilted fabric were certainly produced in and around London at this time. The East India Company records also show that quilted material was imported from the East. Newly available imported calico prints from India became very fashionable and were also most suitable for quilting, which doubtless added to its popularity. Some were imported ready quilted, these were described by a French traveller to India in about 1610, as 'stuffed with cotton, painted and patterned exceedingly prettily'. Others were unsewn, and quilted on arrival in Britain. The quilting on the imported coverlets usually followed the print pattern or was a plain overall trellis; the European products tended to follow an independent pattern and were invariably stuffed with wool instead of cotton.

Soft furnishing in quilted fabrics such as day-time pillow covers, cushion covers and seat covers also became fashionable. The various seventeenth century inventories for Ham House, at Richmond, include many quilted items such as green damask quilted covers for stools, quilted cushions for armchairs, made to match bed furnishings, and 'one piece of quilted hanging steetched with greene collour'.

Underquilts continued to be used throughout the seventeenth and eighteenth centuries. These were generally covered with linen or fustian (a woven fabric with linen warp and cotton weft), though some were doubtless re-used old coverlet quilts of any fabric. Most documentary sources do not differentiate between types of quilt, merely stating '12 quilts of different sort' or '1 old quilt', but others do specify '2 under quilts' or '1 quilt bed'. During the seventeenth century there was positive encouragement for the use of underquilts by writers on health because they were considered more hygienic than featherbeds, which tended to harbour bedbugs. Thomas Tryon, writing in 1691, stated that 'the certain means and way not only to prevent the Generation of this vermin, but also to preserve Health and Strength, is *Straw* or rather *Chaff* Beds, with *Ticks* of *Canvas,* and *Quilts made* of *Wool or Flocks* to lay on them ... But if you are not willing, or so lowly-minded, as to have *Straw* or *Chaff-beds* under your Quilts, then you may have *Flock-beds* with canvas ticking which may be both aired and washed as often as you please'.

Detailed descriptions of coverlet quilts of the seventeenth century are rare, although the covering fabric, usually silk, is often identified in inventories. Satin, calico, fustian, stuff (a light worsted) and sarsenet are also mentioned. Occasionally the colours are also noted. In Ham House there were quilts of red and yellow silk, crimson sarsenet, pink sarsenet and green damask. Plain white quilts seem to have been very common, although many of the surviving quilts from this period are a rather drab colour, presumably the colour described as 'sad' in some inventories. The brighter colours mainly date to the later part of the seventeenth century, when there was doubtless a reaction to the austerity of the Civil War and Cromwellian period. Quilting patterns are unfortunately not described. The motifs used on the few surviving garments and coverlets are similar to those of the following century, namely stylized birds and flowering plants, leaves, chains and diamonds.

Quilting motif, taken from a late seventeenth century quilted jacket

EIGHTEENTH-CENTURY QUILTING

At the beginning of the eighteenth century, it seemed that quilting might be threatened by a ban imposed on the import of the new Indian calicos, which were very suitable and popular for quiltmaking. This was considered sufficiently serious for the professional quiltmakers in London to issue a broadsheet in 1697 protesting against this threat to their livelihood. Despite the ban, however, the demand for the new bright fabrics did not abate. An inventory from Dyrham Park, in Somerset, taken in 1710, lists various calico 'upper quilts', including one specific 'indian printed callico' as well as brightly coloured silk quilts. The high demand coupled with low availability led to a considerable rise in price which ensured that quilts generally remained in upper and middle class homes rather than in the homes of ordinary people. Towards the end of the century, however, quilts began to be listed among the contents of servants' rooms. In an inventory of 1792, the coachman's room at Newby Hall, North Yorkshire, contained a woollen quilt along with a supply of blankets, as did the postillion's and grooms' rooms.

The situation in Wales seems to have been much the same as elsewhere; in 1729 the inhabitants of Picton Castle, Pembrokeshire, Dyfed, owned a number of quilts of silk and calico, as well as two red stuff quilts in the nursery. Stuff is a term which could be used for any fabric but most usually referred to light worsted. The few surviving examples of eighteenth century bed quilts at the Welsh Folk Museum all came from fairly wealthy houses. One, from a large house in the Newcastle Emlyn area of Dyfed, has a yellow silk cover made up of several pieces of silk and a backing of wool and linen. The filling is of fleece, although flock filling was also known at this period. It is well quilted with a complex bordered design with a central medallion, in a style which was later to become regarded as typically Welsh, though at this period was probably fairly general. The medallion centre which often appears on quilt designs may well derive from the designs on the imported Indian chintzes of the period which were frequently printed with a large central medallion bordered by floral motifs. One different type, from north Wales, of the early part of the eighteenth century, is of cream satin embroidered with floral motifs. The quilting is a simple all over trellis design which was common throughout Britain at this period.

Two examples of eighteenth century quilted cushion covers also survive in the Museum collecton. These are both from mansions in the northern part of Wales, one from Golden Grove near Prestatyn in Clwyd and the other from Glansevern near Welshpool, Powys. The Golden Grove cushion is the earlier, and is well quilted with various diamond shapes in a bordered design on a trellis ground. The Glansevern example is dated late eighteenth century and is of cream satin, again with a bordered design.

It is highly significant that all these surviving provenanced examples of quilts are from wealthy houses. Although it may be argued that any quilts in use in poorer homes would not have survived, yet neither is there any documentary evidence that quilts were popular in lower class homes in Wales. One of the aspects of Welsh life remarked upon by the travellers who visited Wales during the eighteenth and nineteenth centuries was the fact that they invariably slept in woollen blankets, often not even making use of linen sheets. Viscount Torrington, on a visit to north Wales in 1793, travelled with his own sheets, and mentions 'no mattress' in Bala and 'a thick double blanket' in Llanrwst. Even the larger houses would have had their share of homespun and woven blankets. The Chirk Castle accounts of 1708 list a payment of 2s. 6d. made to 'old Blanch sometime agoe for spining a pound of wooll to finish ye blanketting', and other payments are listed to a fuller for 'scowring' blankets woven, presumably, within the Chirk estate. Poorer cottagers would have spun their own wool and obtained woven cloth easily in their own locality, without having the

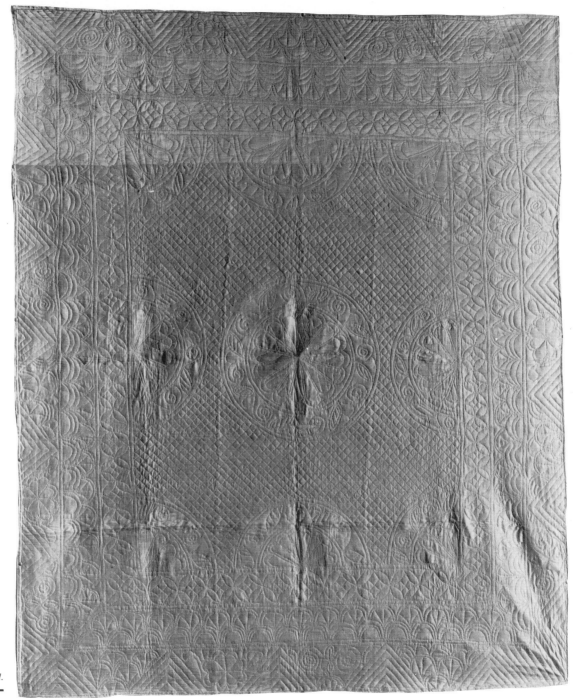

*Yellow silk quilt from
Newcastle Emlyn, Dyfed.*

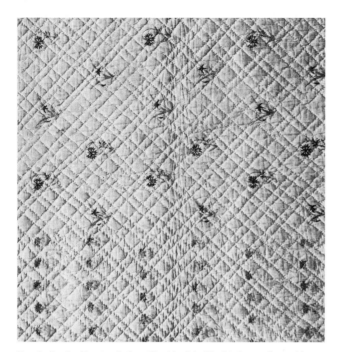

Detail of embroidered quilt from Plas Llanfair, Llanfair-isgaer, Gwynedd.

The later introduction of cheaper roller-printed cotton materials also enabled women lower down the social scale to wear cheerful print dresses and save the scraps for patchwork. As the popularity of quilting and patchwork spread, it seems that quilts gradually disappeared from use in the larger houses and became firmly part of farmhouse and village dwellings.

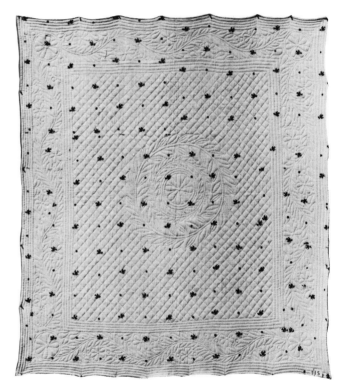

Quilt, late eighteenth century, made from previously embroidered piece of muslin.

expense of buying the fabrics which they would require for quilting. The Chirk Castle accounts do however contain one reference to the use of quilting, though not for bedding; in 1733 there is an entry for: 'A large Elm Coffin lin'd in the inside with a fine white Crape Quilt and ruffle . . .'

Towards the end of the eighteenth century quilting began to move down the social scale. The fashionable and expensive cotton print fabrics had led to a new craze for patchwork among the upper classes. This development is discussed in a later chapter, but patchwork certainly reduced the demand for quilted bedcovers among fashionable society, as did the introduction of Marcella 'quilts', which were woven covers imitating the effect of quilting. These became generally popular later in the nineteenth century, but had been available to wealthier customers from the 1780s. One inventory from a London mansion, Osterley Park, dated 1782, lists a 'white marseills quilt.'

Drawing of quilting pattern of late eighteenth century cushion cover, from Glansevern, Welshpool, Powys.

Drawing of quilting pattern of late eighteenth century cushion cover, from Golden Grove, near Prestatyn, Clwyd.

QUILTED CLOTHING

Quilted petticoats were highly fashionable during the first part of the eighteenth century, but were prohibitively expensive and worn only by the upper and middle classes. One spectacular completely quilted gown of English origin in the Museum of London collection is a cream satin silk sack dress of 1755-65, decorated overall with both wadded and corded quilting, with a matching fully quilted petticoat. Another quilted outfit from the Snowshill Manor collection consists of a quilted hooded jacket with matching petticoat in white satin. Dressmakers were not necessarily required to quilt or design their materials. Quilters in London at this time were producing both ready-quilted lengths of fabric and material marked out with a quilting pattern. Later in the century the fashion spread to the lower classes and to those at the outer reaches of the fashionable world.

By 1714 quilted garments had become so generally worn that in Samuel Richardson's play *Pamela*, the heroine, a lady's maid, was able to consider quilted calico petticoats and 'a good Camblet quilted coat' as perfectly suitable garments for her to wear on her return to life in a small country village. In Richardson's story, Pamela had quilted the petticoats herself, as no doubt a superior lady's maid should. Young ladies of fashion at this period, however, were also still expected to do useful as well as purely decorative needlework. A periodical of the 1740s, *The Female Spectator,* quotes one writer as inveighing against the wholesale production of unwanted and superfluous items of domestic linen and woollen goods by young ladies of fortune. He states 'It always makes me smile when I hear the mothers of fine daughters say 'I always keep my girls at their needle'. One is perhaps engaged upon a gown, another a quilt for a bed, and a third engaged to make a whole dozen of shirts for her father'. This criticism of the encouragement by the mother of industry in her daughters is the beginning of the change in the upper class woman's role to that of the purely decorative, and coincided with the rise in importance of the housekeeper within well-to-do households.

The earliest securely dated quilted garment in the Welsh Folk Museum collection is a baby's christening gown which is probably of Italian origin, made for the christening of Peter Morgan in Milan in 1722 and then brought back to the family home of Golden Grove in Clwyd. This is a standard baby's garment of the late seventeenth and early eighteenth century, being triangular in shape with detachable sleeves. The Italian quilting consists of diamond shapes overall, filled with various flowers, shell patterns and concentric diamonds. Babies' and men's caps also continued to be produced with fine quilting throughout this period.

It was the petticoat, however, which remained generally popular throughout the century and in Wales as well as rural areas of England continued well into the nineteenth century. Some of the eighteenth century petticoats in the collection preserve very attractive quilting patterns. Unlike the stylized designs of many

Baby's christening gown, 1722, from Golden Grove, near Prestatyn, Clwyd.

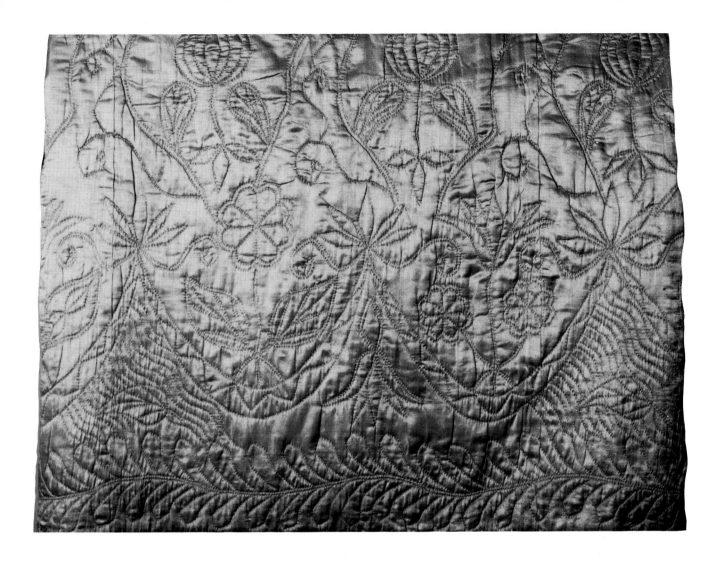

Pink satin petticoat, from the Vale of Glamorgan.

later bedcovers, the motifs around the lower parts of these petticoats are naturalistic flowers, thistles and leaves. One petticoat, of pink satin silk, from the Vale of Glamorgan, has a running feather motif around the hem, which was later to be strongly associated with bed quilts from the north of England. These patterns were intended to be seen, as they were worn with the open-fronted gowns of the period, with only a short embroidered apron covering the upper part. In Wales, the fact that open-fronted gowns were worn as part of rural dress until the middle part of the nineteenth century probably contributed to the survival of the quilted petticoat when it had long ceased to be a fashionable item of clothing. In 1848, a print published by J. C. Rowland representing *Welsh Costumes,* shows an older woman wearing a quilted petticoat beneath her bedgown. Examples of simply quilted petticoats in black satin or fine woollen fabric survive in the museum collection which were worn as late as the 1890s.

Many of these were kept by elderly ladies, who intended them to be burial garments. Some of these are made from ready machine-quilted fabric, while others are well-quilted by hand. In the case of this type of petticoat, the quilting was for warmth rather than display. The two more brightly coloured examples of this later period appear to be made for wear over a crinoline or half-crinoline.

PATCHWORK

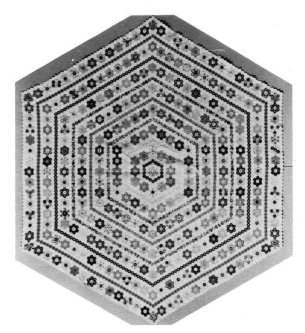

Table cover, circa 1780, from Llwyn Onn, Wrexham, Clwyd.

Although painted Indian chintz fabric had been available throughout the seventeenth century, it was not until the new freedom of the Restoration that the demand for the brightly coloured patterned fabric passed all records. At this time also patterns which conformed to European taste were sent out to India for the craftsmen to copy and adapt. The huge increase in imports during the 1680s began to threaten domestic manufacturers and various steps were taken to limit the imports by legislation. Despite protests from the quiltmakers of London that a ban would be detrimental to their trade, the Government firstly increased import duty and then totally prohibited imports in 1701, and in 1720 banned its use 'in or about any Bed, Chair, Cushion or other household furniture'.

Inevitably this had the perverse effect of making printed calico more desirable to the wealthier households, and a flourishing illicit trade ensured that supplies remained plentiful, though of course at an increased price. The relative scarcity and higher cost of the imported prints caused even small scraps to be saved and the fragments were used to make the first patchwork coverlets. One of the earliest to have survived, dating from about 1708, is at Levens Hall in Cumbria. This consists of octagons and cruciform shapes in Indian chintz applied onto a plain ground. In fact the popularity of the palampores (coverlets comprising a single large chintz panel) and the growing popularity of patchwork reduced the demand for quilted bedcovers for some years. A letter in the India Office Records dated 1687 states 'send noe more quilts of any sort wee having enough to last five or six years, being putt quite out of use by Palempores'.

Quilting did not disappear entirely, but patchwork and applied coverlets certainly became increasingly fashionable during the eighteenth century, being used not only for bedcovers but also hanging curtains and table cloths. One of the earliest pieces in the Welsh Folk Museum collection is a hexagonal patchwork table cover dated *c.* 1780 which consists of radiating rows of small hexagons arranged in a flower garden pattern interlined with rows of smaller hexagons. The overall design has been carefully worked out, and each flower head is well-composed. It is a very good collection of examples of the block-printed cottons available in the Wrexham area of north Wales during the middle part of the eighteenth century. From 1720 the use in Brtain of all cottons printed in England had been banned due to campaigning by the wool and silk producers. This led to a great scarcity, and even when the ban was removed in 1774, the material remained very expensive due to the high rates of duty being levied. This encouraged the thrifty habit of saving scraps of the expensive material and piecing them to form coverlets rather than quilting whole cloth as had been practised previously. The introduction of copperlate printing allowed the production of finely printed panels which were used as the centrepiece of many patchwork coverlets well into the nineteenth century. These

*Quilted patchwork
bedcover, circa
1800-1830, from
Llandeilo, Dyfed.*

Quilted patchwork bedcover, early nineteenth century, from Pembrokeshire, Dyfed.

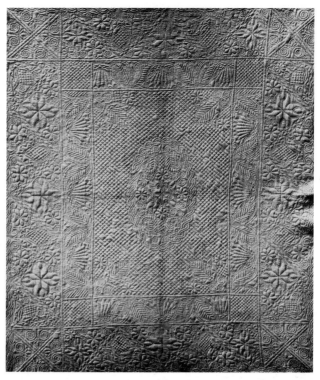

Reverse of bedcover.

frequently copied the 'Indian Tree' designs from the Far East, but royal and political portraits were also produced. One example of a floral print patchwork in the Welsh Folk Museum, made during the first decades of the nineteenth century, has a central panel of flowerheads within a floral wreath surrounded by various rectangular patches in a series of borders. It was also filled with fleece and well quilted. This example was owned by the wife of a maltster in Llandeilo, Dyfed and presumably the product of a reasonably wealthy middle class income. A similar example from the Pembrokeshire area of Dyfed has a central panel of Indian tree pattern with the remainder of the cover a floral print chintz. This is also elaborately quilted, and there has been an attempt to match the quilting pattern to the construction of the cover.

One of the commemorative panels survives on a very large quilted patchwork bedcover, showing a portrait of Queen Caroline, who had gained much popular support during her fight against George IV's attempts to divorce her. The triangular patches are arranged in a fairly haphazard way and the quilting pattern bears no relationship to the patchwork. One particularly fine quilt with a cover of block-printed cottons was made by Mary Lloyd of Cardigan in 1840. This has a central circular printed tree motif set within a field of appliquéd motifs, a wreath of leaves, blue bows and bowls of flowers, the surrounding patchwork consists of rows of block-printed cotton squares. The quilting pattern has been carefully worked to fit in with the appliqué pattern.

*Quilted patchwork bedcover with portrait of Queen Caroline in centre,
circa 1820, from Brecon, Powys.*

Detail of patchwork and appliqué quilt, made by Mary Lloyd of Cardigan, Dyfed, in 1840.

Patchwork cot cover, 1856, belonging to William Hely Llewelyn of Cwrt Colman, near Bridgend, Mid Glamorgan.

After the 1830's the development of roller printing, enabling the mass-production of printed cottons, combined with the abolition of high excise duty in 1831, resulted in the wide availability of cotton print throughout society. From this date surviving examples of patchwork become much more numerous, providing an excellent record of the materials available during the nineteeth century. A cot quilt of 1856 shows the small floral prints which were popular at this time, with a central panel depicting children on a see-saw; this has its young owner's initials and the date written in ink on the lining.

Another type of patchwork which appeared during the first half of the nineteenth century was made from pieces of the closely woven woollen fabric used for military uniforms. These seem to have been made by men, sometimes wounded soldiers or sailors as a form of occupational therapy or else by tailors who had access to the scraps of materials left over from making

uniforms. Both examples in the Welsh Folk Museum collection were made by tailors. One is a well-pieced patchwork with central sunray design, made about 1810 by Andrew Davies of Rhosllanerchrugog, Clwyd. It is edged by a fringe of epaulette trimmings. The other is an extremely complex pictorial bedcover composed of over 4,500 separate pieces, made between 1842 and 1852 by James Williams, a tailor in College Street, Wrexham, Clwyd. As well as various emblems, such as the rose, thistle, leek and shamrock, James Williams included pictorial representations of recent technological wonders such as Telford's Menai suspension bridge and the Cefn viaduct near Ruabon, as well as biblical scenes and animals.

Detail of bedcover, circa 1810, made from scraps of fabric used for military uniforms; from Rhosllanerchrugog, Clwyd.

Detail showing reverse of opposite.

Bedcover made by James Williams, between the years 1842-52, at Wrexham, Clwyd.

*Detail of log cabin patchwork
bedcover from Cardiff, made from
various cotton print and woollen strips.*

Detail of log cabin patchwork bedcover from Llanidloes, Powys, showing the arrangement of strips within one square.

Crazy patchwork made by Jennie A. Jones, a Welsh emigrant in Chicago, USA, 1884.

Turkey red and white patchwork quilt, mid nineteenth century, made by Esther David of Llanfabon, Mid Glamorgan.

Red and white appliqué patchwork, late nineteenth century, from Gelli-Dywyll, Llanbryn-mair, Powys.

As the nineteenth century progressed, other types of patchwork became popular in Wales. As well as the pieced rectangles and hexagons, logcabin and crazy patchwork came into vogue. These were composed of pieces of material sewn onto a base fabric. Logcabin bedcovers consist of strips of fabric arranged to form squares. The fabrics are sometimes printed dress cottons and shirtings or a mixture of the silks, velvets and woollen cloths used in dressmaking in the later part of the century. Through the careful arrangement of the colours into light and dark shades various effective designs could be achieved. Crazy patchwork, despite its name and many badly constructed examples, could also be very well designed and stitched. One particularly fine example, dated 1884, was made by a Welsh immigrant in Chicago, and later sent back to her family in Wales. The cover is made up of nine large squares composed of miscellaneous patches of silks and velvets, some embroidered with floral motifs, the whole bordered by ribbon-embroidered rosebuds.

During the middle part of the nineteenth century there was a vogue for turkey red and white patchwork. This type is represented in the Museum collection by several different styles. There is a well-designed patchwork, made in Llanfabon, Mid Glamorgan and a strip patchwork, unquilted, from Eglwys Bach in Gwynedd which dates from the latter part of the century. A striking quilted appliqué bedcover in red and white, owing something to the American tradition, was made in Llanbryn-mair, Powys, and consists of nine blocks of alternating red and white flowers; the quilting pattern is a double wreath of Welsh feather in the centre and other feather motifs in the border.

24

*Patchwork bedcover, mid nineteenth century, made by the Richards family of
Darowen, Powys.*

Some patchwork was a joint effort by several members of a family, one such is the bedcover from Darowen, Powys, made by members of the Richards family. Another is an unfinished piece of hexagonal patches of cotton print and unbleached calico, on which the tacking stitches and templates are still in place, worked by George Eyre Evans together with his brother and sister at Abergwili, Dyfed, about 1865-70. Yet another type of group patchwork is represented by a bedcover of 1910 made to celebrate the Centenary of Carmel Baptist Chapel at Pontypridd. This includes panels depicting the Chapel in 1810 and 1883 and the landmarks of Pontypridd, with the signatures of members of the chapel embroidered on small pieces of fabric (the members each paid sixpence for their name to be included).

Despite the existence of many well-designed and executed examples of the craft, much of the patchwork produced during the latter part of the nineteenth century was not of the highest standard. Other fabrics which came into use were not quite as suitable for fine work as cotton prints. Later examples include bedcovers made from scraps of furnishing fabric, men's suitings heavy velvets, and flannel acquired from the many woollen mills throughout Wales. Patchwork, like quilting, had moved down the social scale from being a status symbol showing the acquisition of rare Indian chintz, becoming the practice of thrift of the village housekeeper, farmer's wife, or domestic servant in larger houses.

In complete contrast, patchwork today has become the province of the artist rather than a thrift craft. Ironically, new material is now specially purchased and cut into patches in order to create a specific design, and is as likely to hang on a wall in an art gallery as to grace a bed.

NINETEENTH CENTURY QUILTING IN WALES

Once quilts had become removed from the fashionable world, they began to develop in their various localities and to show regional differentiation. It was during the nineteenth century that differences in style began to appear between Welsh quilts and those made in other parts of Britain. Quilting in rural Wales continued and developed very much without outside influences until the middle of the century when many families emigrated to the United States and began to send back examples of American patchwork and quilting. One patchwork covered quilt in the Welsh Folk Museum collection was made by a Mrs Strong of Pittsburg in about 1870, was sent back to her family in Wales and purchased by the Museum in 1946. The cover consists of appliqué floral motifs in red, pink and green cotton print on a white ground and the repeated floral quilting motifs fit the design of the patchwork.

Welsh quilts generally stayed close to the eighteenth century style of a central medallion surrounded by several borders. This changed somewhat towards the end of the century with the use of all over cotton print covers and strippy covers, but the best quilting continued to be produced on plain wholecloth bedcovers. The quilting patterns are certainly seen at their best on these. Patchwork covered quilts, popular from the early years of the nineteenth century, show the quilting well on the reverse side but the patchwork itself effectively hides the quilting craftsmanship. One quilt made in Newport, Dyfed, during the early years of the nineteenth century has its particularly fine quilting pattern visible only on the reverse side. The central motif is of a large flowering pot plant decorated with leaves, spirals, tulips, flowers and hearts on a ground of trellis with a flowering plant in each corner. This motif owes much to the naturalistic style of earlier years. The borders contain motifs such as spirals, veined leaves and hearts which have become associated with Welsh quilts. Most commonly the central motif is circular, as in an example from Ystradfellte in Powys. This has a central circular motif with spirals, surrounded by a circle of four large leaves, with fan shapes in the corners of the central field, which in turn is surrounded by three separate borders of quilting motifs.

Quilted patchwork bedcover, circa 1870, made by a Welsh woman in Pittsburg, Pennsylvania.

Top cover of patchwork quilt, made in Carmarthenshire, Dyfed, circa 1860.

Reverse of above quilt, showing quilting pattern.

Throughout the century, fine quilting continued to be carried out on bedcovers made mainly from cotton. Other types of quilts were made using pieces of flannel in patchwork, but these tended not to be so finely quilted, due to the nature of the material, though the design layout usually adhered to traditional lines. As a testament to the fact that not only the finest examples of quilting survive, quite a number of examples in the Welsh Folk Museum collection are quite poorly made, often with very simple trellis quilting all over, with no attempt having been made at design.

Many of the poorer specimens date from the latter part of the nineteenth century when the popularity of quilting seems to have been on the wane. A contributory factor appears to have been the wide use of brightly coloured cotton print covers which did not show any quilting pattern. Frequently bright red paisley prints were used for both sides of the quilt, and the stitching reverted in many cases to the utilitarian, merely holding the padding in place and contributing nothing to the decoration of the coverlet. The padding itself had also changed by this period. Early Welsh quilts are almost invariably filled with carded fleece, and this continued to be used for filling the best quilts. However, as the element of thrift became more important, many quilts were made using old and worn out blankets as padding and some were filled with all types of fabric scraps. The practical difficulty of stitching through some of the filling fabrics made good work virtually impossible.

However, the craft had not totally degenerated by the end of the century, as is shown by some of the very well made quilts which have survived. Wholecloth quilts continued to be made, and these display all the traditional design elements of earlier work. One example which was made in 1886 as a wedding quilt, has a cotton print top cover and plain reverse. It is very well quilted with a spiral-filled heart surrounded by a circular fan as the central motif. It was made by Mrs Mary Williams, at Berthlwyd Farm, Quakers Yard in Mid Glamorgan and later used by her at Hendre Hall farm, St Mellons, near Cardiff. Other well-quilted bedcovers of the late nineteenth century include one from Henllan Amgoed, near Carmarthen. This has a floral print on one side and plain light brown cotton on the other and has a very complex, well-quilted design. Another has a very secure dating as it has a top cover of cotton fabric printed with Queen Victoria's 1887 Jubilee motif. This is known to have been made by Miss Elizabeth Davies of Pencader, Dyfed, for the wedding of Elizabeth Williams of Llanybydder and John Evans of Llanwenog. Dyfed.

Top cover of patchwork quilt, early nineteenth century, from Ystradfellte, Powys.

Quilt made at Berthlwyd Farm, Quakers Yard, Mid Glamorgan in 1886.

Quilt made at Penclippin Farm, Henllan Amgoed, Dyfed, late nineteenth century.

QUILTMAKERS

Quilts were produced both by professional quilters and by housewives for their own use. Whereas the home-made quilts of the eighteenth century had been the product of the leisure hours of upper class ladies, nineteenth century quilting was often necessary thrift for poorer housewives. In rural south and west Wales every girl was expected to have stock of at least six quilts as part of her dowry, such items being considered essential for the setting-up of a home. Sometimes special marriage quilts were made, incorporating heart motifs, but dowry quilts are not usually distinguishable by any special patterns or motifs.

Since the quilting frames were so large, they were usually set up for work after the morning meal, then rolled up and stored away before the preparation for the evening meal. In larger farmhouses, with several rooms, it was possible to leave the frame set up until the work was completed. Young girls usually learned the craft from watching their mothers or grandmothers at work and helping by threading needles. In this way 'traditional' designs and patterns were passed from one generation to the next. When the girls became more proficient at needlework, they would work alongside their elders, sometimes as many as six women working on a quilt at one time.

There were two categories of professional quilter— the village quilter, who was often also a dressmaker, and the itinerant quilter. Itinerant quilters worked in the more remote rural areas and travelled from farm to farm in the same way as other craftsmen such as saddlers and tailors. All the materials were usually provided by the farmer, including occasionally the quilting frame, though the quilter often travelled with her own frame. Mrs Priscilla Roberts, an octogenarian in 1953, recalled an old lady in Garthbeibio near Llanfair Caereinion, Powys 'who went from farm to farm, carrying on her back a quilting frame. She spent

Village quilters at Solva, Dyfed 1928.

Village quilters at Solva, Dyfed 1928.

a month or more at the different farms, sewing, mending and quilting' (*Montgomeryshire Collections*, Vol. 53). This is one of the few references to quilting in the northern part of Wales, though the craft must have been widely practised there during the nineteenth century. Other areas of scattered farmsteads which lent themselves to this form of travelling craftswoman were the old counties of Cardiganshire, Carmarthenshire and Pembrokeshire. In the Borth area of Cardiganshire, Mrs Katy Lewis remembers that her grandmother kept a quilting frame in the farmhouse for the use of the travelling quilter, though she never quilted herself.

The invaluable information collected from quilters by Mavis FitzRandolph during the 1920's as part of her work for the Rural Industries Bureau seems to indicate that there were quite a number of women making a living as itinerant quilters during the latter years of the nineteenth century, though the practice had died out around the time of the First World War. Usually they were paid on a daily rate, which varied from sixpence up to as much as three shillings during the 1890s and early 1900s, free lodging and food were also provided. The rates were roughly equivalent to those of travelling dressmakers who also occasionally included quilting among their skills. Unfortunately, few professionally-made quilts have their makers documented, unlike those made within the family. However, one quilt in the Museum collection is known to have been made by an itinerant quilter in the Brecon area of Powys. This has a patchwork cover of red and white hexagons and a traditional quilting pattern of central floral roundels with an outer border of chain motif. Another, with a pink sateen cover, dated 1890, is known to have been made at Trefigin Farm in the parish of Monington, Pembrokeshire by a seamstress from Cardiganshire who visited annually to make and repair clothing and bedding.

In the case of village quilters, customers brought their own fabric and paid for the work per quilt. The rate of work varied considerably, but one a fortnight seems to be generally accepted as the average for one quilter, though many village quilters worked with an apprentice. Since most of the information about this period has been gathered from oral testimony it is difficult to calculate rates of pay for these women,

Simple patchwork cover of quilt made at Ponterwyd, Dyfed in about 1882.

though an average payment of six to eight shillings per quilt from about 1890 to 1900 seems to be indicated by information collected by Mavis FitzRandolph.

None of the quilts in the Museum collection are conclusively documented as the work of a village quilter, though one which may be is a patchwork covered quilt said to have been made by one 'Fani Fach Siân William' at Ponterwyd, Dyfed in about 1882. This has a quilting pattern of a central circular motif filled with leaves, surrounded by borders of concentric circles, spirals and diamonds. It seems that the standard of work varied considerably, with some quilters such as Mari Jones of Panteg, Dyfed, having a reputation for very fine quilts while others worked more quickly, doing rougher work with simple patterns and large motifs.

With the growth of the South Wales Coalfield during the nineteenth century, many families from the rural areas moved to the industrial valleys. This brought quilters to the valley towns, who were then able to swell the family income by quilting for their neighbours. Due to a general scarcity of spare cash, quilt clubs were formed and a system of payment by instalments was instituted. A number of these quilt clubs still survived in south Wales as late as 1928. Mrs Lace, a quilter in Aberdare, who took part in the Quilting Exhibition of 1951 at the Welsh Folk Museum, kept a notebook detailing orders for quilts which she made during 1907, a year when there was a long coal strike. Her total earnings for the year were ten guineas for making twenty six quilts.

Mrs Lace and Mrs Olivia Evans demonstrating quilting at an exhibition at the Welsh Folk Museum in 1951.

DECLINE AND REVIVAL

A number of professional quilters were still at work during the early years of the twentieth century, notably village quilters in west Wales and club quilters in the industrial valleys. Women also continued to quilt for their own families, and some very nicely quilted examples still survive from the pre-war period. After the 1914-18 war, the market for hand-made quilts began to wane even in Wales, where they had retained their popularity longer than in many areas of Britain. This was partly due to the easy availability of mass-produced counterpanes such as the woven cotton covers and marcella 'quilts' which had been popular since the middle of the nineteenth century. By the end of the nineteenth century eiderdowns were becoming fashionable, as were woollen jacquard-weave coverlets which were available from woollen mills throughout Wales, and by the 1930s the candlewick bedspread had made its appearance. Quilts came to be regarded as rather old-fashioned, and the use of busy printed fabrics meant that the handwork was not so valued as it had formerly been.

There were also social factors at work; during the First World War many young girls did war work in the Land Army, munitions factories and other jobs previously done by men. They were not at home learning such skills as quilting from their mothers, nor did they need or wish to earn a poor living from their needles. Wartime shortages of materials also hit the professional quiltmakers, though there was no severe rationing as later occurred during the Second World War. The post-war flood of army surplus blankets may also have affected the quilters' business, as it certainly did the business of many of the woollen mills of rural Wales.

During the post-war years there were two positive efforts to encourage the revival of the craft. One was in the area of amateur quilters, through the encouragement provided by the Women's Institutes who did much to promote handicrafts including embroidery, rug making and quilting, most especially in the northern counties of England. However, the main impetus which led to a revival in quilting was a scheme instituted by the Rural Industries Bureau in 1928 which aimed to encourage small craft industries in depressed areas. In the case of crafts such as blacksmithing or pottery, this involved giving advisory help, but with quilting a little more practical assistance was required. During 1928 Mavis FitzRandolph traced individual village quilters, and although much of the work was poorly done using cheap gaudy materials, she found many of the women were capable of better work given better materials and a rate of pay which enabled them to spend the time needed to produce work of a high standard. Financial help was therefore provided so that good quality materials could be used, and orders were obtained through commercial galleries in London.

Quilt made in 1906 by Mrs Phoebe Walters of Bancyfelin, Dyfed.

Quilter demonstrating at one of the Rural Industries Exhibitions held at David Morgan department store during the 1930s.

It soon became apparent that although there were good quilters looking for orders in south Wales, there were not enough of them in the industrial valleys capable of the high standard of work required. Since it was the depressed mining communities which the scheme was intended to help, it was decided to organize classes, taught by the most accomplished quilters in the area.

Several groups were set up in the south Wales valleys, at Porth in the Rhondda, Aberdare in the Cynon Valley, and Abertridwr in the Rhymney Valley among others. The work of the Porth group became especially well-known, mainly due to the excellence of their teacher Miss Jessie Edwards. An example of their work was presented to the National Museum in 1933 by the Rural Industries Bureau to join what was at that time a small and unrepresentative collection of quilts and patchwork. The following years, up to and including the Second World War, were to see much active collecting of quilts by the Museum.

One of the groups which still has surviving members is that which was formed at Abertridwr. The girls who took part in this scheme were particularly young, around nineteen to twenty years of age. Other groups included established quilters who were therefore older women. Although at least ten girls started in the class, only four remained to become the Abertridwr group— Gwen Stone, Nest and Marion Smith and Katy Lewis. According to Mrs Lewis, their teacher Miss Owen was a hard taskmaster, though an excellent teacher. She was a dressmaker, whose mother had been a quilter at Porth in the Rhondda. There was, therefore, a direct link with traditional Welsh quiltmaking. Mrs Phillips, a local woman and aunt to two of the girls, was secretary of the group; she liaised with the Rural Industries Bureau, arranged for the provision of materials and it was she who despatched the finished articles to London. Other local women, such as the colliery manager's wife and local shopkeepers, also assisted the group by obtaining orders both in the district and from contacts in Cardiff. The standard of work demanded by the London outlets was very high. Miss Muriel Rose of the Little Gallery in particular insisted on good needlework and well-designed quilts. The girls learned to do fine stitching and to use traditional patterns to form their own designs. After the classes were completed they worked as a co-operative.

Miss Jessie Edwards, teacher of the Porth group of quilters, shown holding a quilt which later came into the collections of the Welsh Folk Museum.

According to Katy Lewis, a full size quilt would be completed by two women in a fortnight. When the four worked on one quilt together they must have been able to complete a quilt per week. It was quite a co-operative effort, with the four girls marking and pinning the quilt onto the frame, designing the pattern together, and finally stitching the quilts; 'When we quilted, the four of us, and we had a big frame, it was right across the room; we had a trestle; Marion and Gwen sat on one side and Nest and I on the other; it was divided into four; you couldn't see where one had finished and the other started; we all worked out the design between us, we just did it as we went along'.

For this work, they were paid 1/6d a square foot for the quilting by the R.I.B. with the Bureau providing their materials. This rate later rose to 2/4d a square foot. In the case of a local order, they would receive the price of the quilt, which might by anything from four pounds to about nine pounds, depending on the size and materials used. For example, the price of a six foot by seven foot silk quilt, quoted in a notebook in the possession of Mrs Lewis, was six guineas, whereas the price quoted for a similar quilt, in a pricelist of R.I.B. quilts in the Little Gallery, was eleven guineas in the 1930s.

The scheme definitely succeeded in raising the standard of quilting produced and created a new awareness of traditional patterns. Mavis FitzRandolph noted that Welsh women in particular produced fresh ideas based on the old patterns. Although the women were producing for a luxury market outside their own locality, there was awareness of their skill locally and a demand arose for quilting evening classes and summer schools. Many of the quilters taught in these classes, which provided them with some income when the scheme came to an end in 1939 after the outbreak of the war.

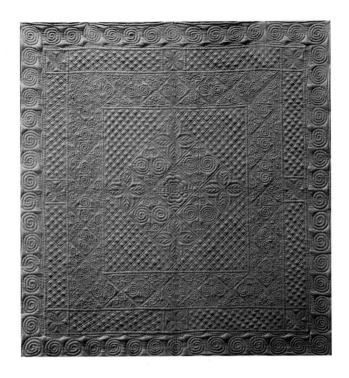

Quilt made by the Porth quilters in 1933 and presented to the National Museum of Wales by the Rural Industries Bureau.

THE POST-WAR PERIOD

Although the Bureau scheme foundered after the onset of the Second World War, due mainly to the wartime rationing of materials, several individuals continued to quilt and taught at night classes. Quilting as a craft industry, however, seems to have disappeared at this time, as the demand for luxury goods ceased during the war and immediate post-war period. There were, however, attempts to revive the craft. In 1950, a quilting conference was held at the newly established Welsh Folk Museum. Mavis FitzRandolph was invited

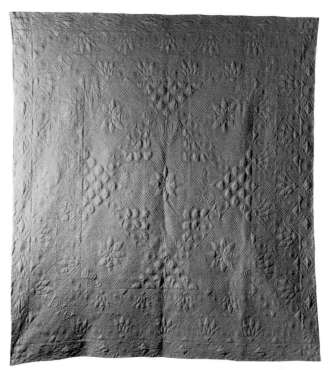

Quilt made by Miss Emiah Jones of Cross Hands, Dyfed, which won first prize at the 1951 Exhibition.

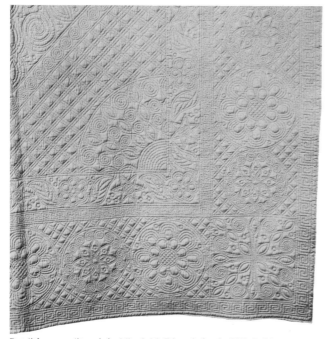

Detail from a quilt made by Miss J. M. Edwards for the 1951 Quilting Exhibition held at the Welsh Folk Museum.

and other interested parties locally, including a number of quilters who had worked under the R.I.B. scheme and who were at that time teaching. As a result of this meeting, an exhibition and competition were organized for the following year, to be held at the Welsh Folk Museum. This attracted work from the best quilters still working in south Wales. Jessie Edwards made a beautiful, immaculately worked white quilt for the exhibition, which came into the Museum collection some ten years later. The competition was won by a very complex piece of work made by Emiah Jones of Cross Hands in Dyfed. Another prize winner was Mrs Katy Lewis of the Abertridwr group. The exhibition consisted of a selection of old quilts and quilted petticoats from the Welsh Folk Museum collection together with the finest examples of modern Welsh quilting.

*General views of the 1951
exhibition, held in the old
banqueting hall in the grounds
of St Fagans Castle.*

Despite the high standard of work and the interest caused, no real progress towards a true revival was made. Both Jessie Edwards and Katy Lewis, and a number of others, continued to teach, but women were no longer keen to take on the task of making large bed quilts and the products of the post-war era are mainly confined to cushion covers, cot covers and dressing gowns.

One example of an unfinished dressing gown in the Museum is a product of the Merthyr Tudful class held by Jessie Edwards. This displays all the stages of construction, including a portion in which the quilting has been completed, and a piece still attached to the frame, with the pattern marked in chalk but unstitched.

The latest quilting revival, which began during the 1970s under the strong influence of a very lively tradition in the United States, and encouraged by the formation of the Quilters Guild, has resulted in quilts and particularly patchwork being made in large numbers once more, though the craft is now practised as a leisure activity rather than a craft industry.

Parts of an unfinished red satin dressing gown, made during quilting classes in Merthyr Tydfil during the 1950s.

QUILTING TECHNIQUE

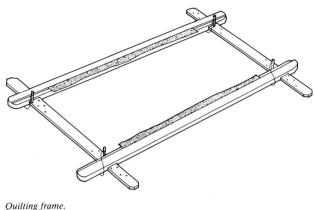

Quilting frame.

When stitching a quilt it is essential that all three layers are kept taut and even. For this purpose, a quilting frame was used. This was a simple piece of equipment, often home-made, which consisted of two long wooden 'runners', to which webbing was tacked, and two shorter 'slides' which slotted into the runners to form an adjustable rectangle. The runners varied in length according to the size of the quilt to be made, and could be over two and a half metres long. A small item such as a cushion cover could be made on a fixed rectangular frame similar to a picture frame (indeed it has been known for picture frames to be used for this purpose).

For a wholecloth quilt, the fabric was first seamed together, with a full panel in the centre, and the seams to the side. Seams were usually backstitched by hand even in the more recent quilts, but some quilters did use a machine for this part of the work. The halfway point and quarters were then marked as an aid to centring the fabric on the frame and later laying out the design. The next step was to stitch or pin the edge of the bottom layer of fabric onto the webbing of the runners, then the other side was rolled up until it was the correct width for the slides to be attached. These were then held in position by wooden pegs and the side edges of the fabric fastened by means of tapes, to the slides. The material was thus held taut on all sides. At this stage the padding was arranged in an even layer over the base fabric. If wool was used, it was well washed and carded by hand. Other poorer types of filling such as an old blanket, or even discarded clothing were also used. This latter type of padding produced a less even filling and was much more difficult to stitch. The modern alternative is polyester wadding.

Once the filling was in place, the top cover was pinned or sewn into position on the frame so that it too was held tightly in position. The surplus material at one side was rolled up and usually covered with a cloth to keep it clean. The quilt was then ready for planning the design. There is no evidence that ready-marked fabric was bought for quilting, as was the practice in the north of England where there were a number of well-known professional quilt markers.

The design was usually marked from the centre working outwards. Various methods were used to mark the fabric. Tailor's chalk was preferred by most Welsh quilters, while in the north of England marking the cloth by pricking with a needle was more general. A collection of different-sized rulers was part of the quilter's equipment; these were used for marking edges and borders as well as some of the in-fill patterns such as trellis. Many of the patterns were only roughly marked out by sticking pins into the fabric, the intricate detail being stitched freehand. Templates were used for marking some motifs, these were cut out of paper or cardboard, although occasionally domestic articles such as saucers and plates were used directly on the fabric. However, it was not uncommon for quilters to draw motifs freehand. Mrs Katy Lewis has described how she marked her design: 'You'd mark the outline and sometimes you'd fill it freehand or you used the template. There's the rose—to mark the rose you get a circle, then that would come from the centre to (make) the scallop and you mark it round, every one [ie every petal]. With the squares [trellis], you mark them all with a ruler, but when you're doing a filling-in stitch, such as going around the edge of the rose, you don't get a bigger rose to put there, you just mark it with the chalk free hand. It's surprising how you get the eye to get it straight, you get it even'.

Once the working area was marked, stitching could begin. Although backstitch was used on some early quilts, in the main running stitch was used for quilting. The needle had to pass through all three layers of material with each stitch. The quilters sat with one hand under the frame and would 'feel every stitch', that is feel every needle through and push the point back up with their finger. The constant pricking made the skin on the fingers of the underneath hand very hard. A thimble was used on the upper hand, to push the needle through the fabric, but could not be used on the underneath hand because of the necessity to feel that the needle had pierced all three layers.

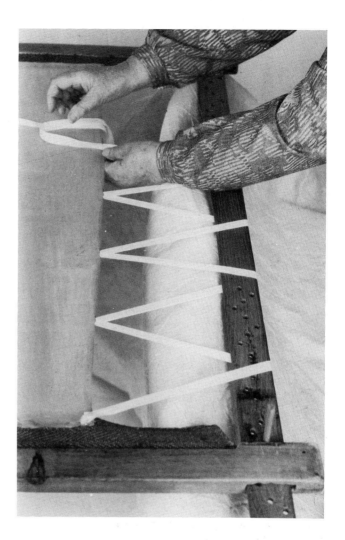

Mrs. Katy Lewis, one of the Abertridwr group of quilters, pinning the first piece of fabric on to the webbing of the frame.

Taping the sides of the fabric, having put the slides into position.

Approximately five stitches would be taken on each needle before the thread was pulled right through. Each piece of thread was started off with a knot which was worked through the top layer so that it was hidden between the layers, then often a single backstitch was worked before beginning the running stitch. Stitches had to be even both to produce a good effect and so that the top and bottom of the quilt were equally quilted. Very fine stitching sometimes pulled the threads of the fabric; an ideal average was approximately six to eight stitches to the inch. Quilters had to be able to stitch evenly whether working towards or away from themselves, working a circle or spiral is particularly difficult. The quilters were not able simply to turn the frame around as with a small embroidery frame.

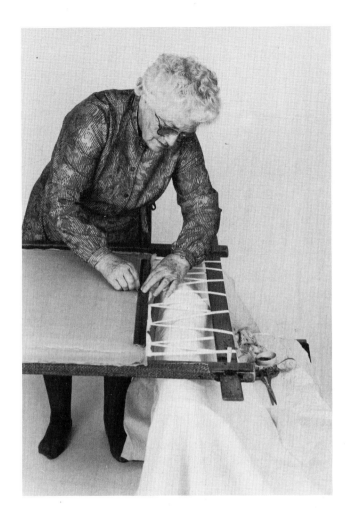

Placing the top cover in position over the filling.

Marking the border with a ruler.

Marking the central motifs, using templates.

Stitching the quilt, using the left hand to push the needle back up through the fabric.

Gathering several stitches on the needle.

When the portion stretched in the frame was finished, it was rolled up and the next part treated in the same way, until the whole quilt was completed. The quilt was then removed from the frame and the raw edges finished off by simply turning them in, pinning, and sewing around with two rows of running stitch. Later quilts were sometimes finished with a frill or with piping.

The finished cot quilt.

QUILTING PATTERNS

Many different patterns were used on Welsh quilts, each quilter using her own variations so that no two quilts were ever exactly the same. There were usually three main pattern elements—large motifs, infill patterns and border patterns. A few of the quilts in the Museum collection have a single repeated design worked all over the quilt, but this is less common than the standard arrangement of a large central motif surrounded by one or more borders. The overall repeated design was most frequently used for a quilt with a patchwork cover in which case the quilting motif was worked to fit with the patchwork pattern.

Bordered designs, however, form the vast majority of quilts of all periods in the Welsh Folk Museum collection. The central motifs were sometimes floral or variations on a circle, and often incorporated heart and leaf shapes. The lover's knot which appears on many north of England quilts does not seem to have been so popular in Wales. The naturalistic motifs which appear on the petticoats of the eighteenth century do not seem to have been used on bed quilts, although one unusual quilt made in Pembrokeshire, Dyfed, during the 1840s depicts a pot containing a large flowering plant as its central motif.

The central motif is set within a rectangular field, almost invariably delineated by two rows of plain running stitch. The four corners of this field usually have fan-shaped quarter motifs matching the central motif. The background is generally filled with a plain infill pattern. The remaining border or borders are then filled with a mixture of smaller motifs and infill patterns.

References to the actual motifs used in quilting can be very confusing, as different terminology is used by each quilter. In addition, not all patterns had a name, but names have been created by later writers for descriptive purposes. The most common infill pattern is one of lines crossing each other at right angles. This is known variously as trellis, plaid and diamonds. It is sometimes stitched with double or triple lines. If these lines are woven above and below each other, then it produces a pattern known as basket-weave or lattice. Patterns could be named after the utensils which were used as templates. For example, the popular infill design of overlapping circles was most frequently called wine glass, or occasionally tea cup pattern.

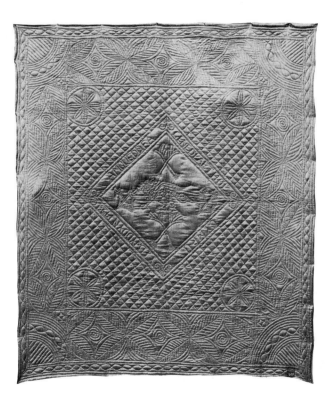

Quilt made especially for the National Museum of Wales in 1929 at Gelli, Rhondda, Mid Glamorgan. The unusual central motif is surrounded by typical elements of Welsh quilting—trellis, beech leaves, spirals and chain.

Spiral-filled hearts from a quilt made at Henllan Amgoed, Dyfed.

so we just did others—circles, leaves, paisley, rose and hearts and then you made up your patterns by interwining them'. Patterns passed on from mother to daughter or quilter to apprentice survived the centuries to be finally adopted as 'Welsh' patterns during the quilting revival of the 1920s and 1930s.

This confusion of pattern names also applies to the small border motifs. There were many 'family patterns' used by quilters which were in fact widely used, but merely possessed a particular name within that family. Many of the motifs were based on the circle, various flower and rose patterns, the spiral or 'snail creep', and shell and wave patterns. Particularly popular in Wales was the beech leaf, used in various combinations, the spiral and also a teardrop shape known as the Welsh pear or paisley motif. Feather motifs, which were popular in the north of England, do not appear on many of the Welsh quilts in the Museum collection, though running feather designs do appear on some eighteenth century specimens. During the nineteenth century there is no evidence that there was any conscious adoption of particularly Welsh patterns, though this distinction was certainly made during the revival in the twentieth century. Mrs Katy Lewis has commented that in the Abertridwr group they used many motifs 'But not the continuous feather, we didn't do a lot of the feather at all, because that was Durham,

Central flowering plant motif from a Pembrokeshire quilt of the early nineteenth century.

Half pattern showing heart motifs, spirals and fans, with curved leaves in the border, from a marriage quilt made at Quakers Yard, Mid Glamorgan, circa 1886.

Quarter pattern drawn from a wholecloth cotton quilt, nineteenth century, possibly from Newcastle Emlyn, Dyfed.

Quarter pattern showing a typical combination of large veined leaves and spirals, from a quilt made circa 1900.

Quarter pattern showing the complex closely stitched quilting in Miss J. Edwards's quilt made for the 1951 exhibition.

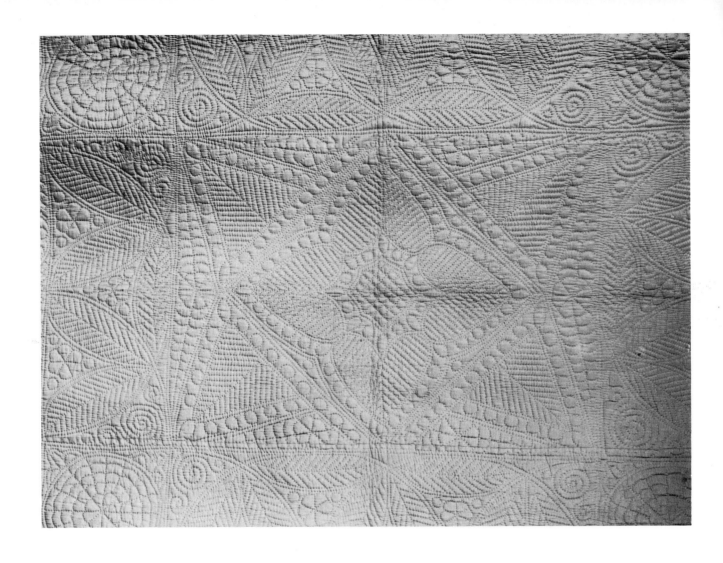

Arrangement of heart motifs on a quilt made in Maesteg, Mid Glamorgan,
during the mid 1920s.

Further Reading

R. E. Allan, *North Country Quilts and Coverlets from Beamish Museum* (1987)

I. E. Anthony, 'Quilting and Patchwork in Wales', *Amgueddfa* (1972), pp.2-15

S. Betterton, *Quilts and Coverlets from the American Museum in Britain* (1972) and *More Quilts and Coverlets* (1989)

A. Colby, *Patchwork Quilts* (1965), Batsford

A. Colby, *Quilting* (1972), Batsford

M. FitzRandolph, *Traditional Quilting* (1954), Batsford

D. Osler, *Traditional British Quilts* (1987), Batsford

J. Rae, *The Quilts of the British Isles* (1987), Constable